AF430407

FOR THE WILLING

≈

POEMS

KRISTIN BERGER

NIGHTJAR POETRY PRESS

2024

FOR THE WILLING

for Alice & Margot

FOR THE WILLING

FORWARD

When the poems in this collection first started to emerge, my oldest child was six months old and had just started to nap predictably. I could write while they slept and try and catch up on each moment, which felt both hurried and suspended, time doing its elastic thing. I wrote as they learned to crawl and walk, and wake up from naps sweaty headed, finding me at my desk, climbing onto my lap. I wrote while pregnant with my second child, and only because they were two weeks overdue was I able to send the manuscript to a contest. That chapbook became my first book, and like all children, it grew, evolved, and moved out into the world for others to meet and get to know.

More than twenty years later, and with that first book out of print, I realized this was the perfect opportunity to revisit the poems and make a few necessary edits and additions—update genders (they/them instead of she/hers and he/him), correct some ungraceful line breaks, and add a couple poems from where I sit now as a mother with an intermittent empty nest. Nostalgia is a shifting landscape, terrarium, river delta—every time you look at it, the species of memory slip and reveal something unexpected. Children grow out of the poems and can never really be known again in the same way. You grow as a parent of adult and nearly adult humans who have transitioned into identities which align with their hearts. You do not forget the wonder that rooted both your children's lives and the poems, which continue to reach for you, year after year, at every slight turn. It is still there, low and near, still rustling, if you are willing to reach back, and forward, for all of it.

Kristin Berger
April 2024

THINK OF A KITCHEN TABLE

"Think of a kitchen table then," he told her, "when you're not there."
—Virginia Wolfe, To the Lighthouse

To have a child sleeping in the house above you while you're writing
at the kitchen table is to be wrapped in a light blanket that warms
the panes of morning. Their breathing is easy, and so is yours, finally.
You're not ready for the empty nest. The smallness of their hands,
as they were, tugs at you. You understand, now, how mothers can stare
out windows for hours, then pick themselves up and go bake a cake.

There was no offramp, or at least if there was one, you were driving
too fast to exit as if you were driving blind. How did I get here?
Did I really make those turns? The rain falls and bookmarks the minutes.
You can hold and hold, but look out the window and see that lightened
bank of clouds suggesting a break? Suggesting day, suggesting time.

The rain will come, and the child will wake. The child the same height
as you without shoes, will look you in the eyes, hopefully, and say,
good morning, how did you sleep?

MOONKILLING

"o what will become of the world, the moon
never dies without cause ...
throw your sticks, help out."
                    —from *Moon Eclipse Exorcism*, the Alsea Tribe

Moving in shadow tonight, beyond the earth,
the moon rises red above a spring-shot world.
Our gray, dark valley. It eclipses the call
of pheasant startled from its cover of thick reeds,
wings and tail scraping the horizon, a frightened arc
between bird and the earth's insistence leashing it down.

The moon pulls at all waters in all bodies
waiting for a signal—that this is the night to love,
to stand clear of trees and dance, to push life out.
Cloaked by cloudy sky-scrim, the moon goes blank.
It turns from field, lake, eyes. As if we are no longer
the center of the universe.

In the old days, when the moon crimsoned,
it was thought all rivers would run as blood
and life would end. Frogs empty their throat-songs
into the darkness. The moon-albedo strengthens
like our prayers eroding the bead.

There is always another chance, another revolving
away from the past, bathed in black, to a slate clean,
yet pock-marked and old. A weathered returning.
Our third eye watches the world, all our births
and the smoke of our fires, above all our scramblings
and our attempts at flight from such a small, hot rock.

LEVELING THE YARD AT DUSK

Under the old plum tree, the earth is swept black,
plucked of leathery weeds and last year's spent pits
except for white blossoms falling, some whole
like loosened charms—stars of snow
drifting across the soil.

I take the split-handled hoe and tease clumps
and petals into a place a small foot could walk upon,
evenly, into an idea of grass. Shake the roots
of spearmint and though I cannot see, I trust
the filaments are releasing dirt back to worms
worrying over their lost tunnels.

Frogs join the song of hoe tripping on sunk rock,
the planet now dark. Stars begin to make their way.
They will shed their lantern husks, trade their worn
white light for a sturdy green promise—
what was for what might be, as soon
as my back is turned.

DREAMING YOU WHILE DRIVING THE COLUMBIA
for Alice

Down from arid wheat land, a black basalt ridge seams the world together.
Bunch-grass shoulders the soft earth that slopes, with an ancient arching
to the river. Windsurfers skid—damselflies winging a brittle brilliance
across wide water, for each other. Against my weathered and slumped bones
you rest. Your spine rocks within. Lovely pearls, strung in sleep
mapping a bare country, a calcifying will strengthening under
the moon's pale belly pressed against a taut, empty blue.
You crave to crest into your first breath, from gill to wing
in one ambitious flip below the cage of my ribs.
We skirt cliff-bottoms, speed with metallic grace
as lasting as our wake along the black backbone
of beginning. Holding river currents
to their course, towards the mouth
and the bar, towards our
eventual unraveling.

STAKING THE TRELLIS

You wouldn't expect that at the time of magnolias
a divorce could also be forcing itself open
into otherwise quiet lives, like seeds halving
at midnight, when love is supposed to bloom
like a clichéd song. All the neighborhood birds
hover at the edge of the compost you have tilled
into the bed, rich and curling with worms.
The crows, even higher, clot the clouds
with their hawk-temper and oiled hunger.
They know that the hard white peas just planted,
covered by the thinnest humus, must climb
the ladder you have laced—they gather as you stand
back from the harp-work of jute and guard
the empty places wavering in the garden,
wait for the marriage of vine to rung,
light to leaf, for some green will
to continue the blinding
search upward.

ULTRASOUND

Revolving out from darkness
your bone white face turns
to me. You are the fiercest shroud
of baby fat, lanugo invisible
above your heart cupped
by slivered ribs keeping
everything at bay, including me,
who surrounds. Bird wrists.
Pearly backbone. Static visions
of you come clear moving up
to the surface of your sky.

The dimmed room cools.
Outside, heat flares from pavement
to an open, un-blinking blue.
I lie, a victim of the moment,
surrendering our water-drowsed
bodies to the black corners.
You turn away.

Safety in our little enclosed ways.
Circling, denning down
for a twinned sleep.

THE POEM IS THE YEAR

My womb is the small secret page,
the right words dividing, scrolling to life.

January, I crochet a blanket covering my lap,
then fall asleep. Rain swims gray and light.

February. A candle. The table set.
The love between. The heartbeat.

March is an ocean storm, logs rolling,
beach-etching. I wake up.

In April, I de-robe and laugh.
I eat yogurt and begin to consider *Baby*.

By May, I wear the mother-clothes and show the world
the old backyard roses that open pink and sharp-scented.

In June, nipples darken, and I sleep the long dreams,
day and night, of a woman being visited.

July, a cool desert creek plays with the roots of pines.
Baby whispers to the stars, my belly their tent.

August. The heat. The tomatoes.
The whale swallowed by woman.

September stretches and we harvest and feast.
Labor at sunset on the Equinox. I push. You pull.

The child finds their way, my breasts leak gold.
The poem, flesh-made, glistening, is unbound.

AFTER BIRTH

In the expanse of the bath, I float.
Water and sunlight scribe white walls.
The ocean's whir this far inland, is memory
of another water that filled me, cured me
with brine, while a current of blood
orbited its own small, lopsided planet.
Swimming there, safely, in saltwater
and darkness, was the universe of *Them*.

Together we navigated the lessons of bore tides,
of becoming the opening through which all must
eventually funnel. Soft bones collapsed
between the mother-bones. Our tether pulsed.
They slipped away, found dry land.

My hand rests on the isosceles of hip and navel
framing the island uninhabited, steaming pink,
above the bright water.

WHEN THE MOON FLOATS UNNOTICED

and the wind is directionless you wake at 3 a.m.
to a spring snow wedding cherry blossoms
like a thin lace veiling stunned and starved bees
and watch out the window as the only streetlamp
casts its gold glance on the trajectory of the storm,
the last moment before flakes stall on car hoods
like the chance-witness to comet dust scattering
through clouds, the hope of a dream behind the lid,
something to believe, someone to wake
for their first milky light.

GROUNDED

Meant to live like a bird, wings tucked
into the cleft neatly next to beating
breast, a barbed cage containing
this restlessness for the last grub
under a dank rock, the last meal
before joining millions in their quaking
lullaby, wings crooning noon
and night, leaving the holly, the currant,
cones that clot boughs packed
with seeds like secrets as if
birds needed bribes, a keep-here
song, were my kin, as if
these birds knew to return
to the ferns beneath my window
that I waited, thumbing crackers
left in dry pockets, wings folded
heart drumming, gaining strength.

JANUARY AT THE DUCK POND

The signs are there if you pace yourself, look
low under the beaks of mergansers slipping
beneath drowned willow—what you'd expect,
the light at the same angle, then look again.

No one here maps the way. The next moment unfolds,
smallish and surprising as the year's first snow stars
pearling the nubby roots of rhododendrons.
Daphne musk haunts the path, an old story.

You would never expect it to come back to you,
soil gracing its way to life. But look low,
mallards rustling the dry duff near
the booted foot of your child, who reaches
with a fistful of corn for anything
willing to come close.

RUMOR

There's a story shared every spring of a boy
who wanders his neighbors' yards at dawn—
spotted by the bachelor sipping his coffee
and the grandmother crumbling bread
in her palms for robins and mourning doves
halted at the borders. Flower beds quiver,
part, and the boy emerges, wet webs crowning
his head. The gaudy tips of daffodils
push up out of his shirt neck, fill
his back pockets. He cannot carry
enough home, this swelling gold
on his slight frame, this sun
at his throat.

THEY WANT TO TASTE EVERYTHING

Strawberries send sister-shoots across the path
leading the baby to each spectacular fruit
they can reach, rain-taut and dimpled,
a connect-the-dot game for the willing.

They bury their face in the lavender bush
as content as the morning's fat bees.
An earthworm entertains from my palm,
wiggling the Good Earth Dance.

The world is edible. They want it all
at their lips, devours milk and sunlight
just sitting in dewed pajamas,
their whole body a taproot.

Learning to use thumb and finger,
they pick a path through desire.
For now, their fists are berry stained.
Grass blooms between each knuckle,
the earth, compacted, snug inside.

LEARNING THEIR NAMES AS THEY GO

An inverted "V" below the nose
is the sign we use to say *Walrus*—
two tusks beneath scruffy cheeks
like an old man with kind eyes
waiting to be noticed,
an illustration in a child's book
full of disappearing wonders—
beluga, narwhal, murre—
their names spoken
like ice-numbed mantras
that we also learn, more words
than species, more ways of saying
the thing that is becoming
less than paper and ink.

But they love him, Walrus.
How could they not, floating
on his thin berg towards the hot,
open sea? Love at first sight
and pointed out on each page,
his toothy simplicity mirroring
their mouth still accumulating pearls,
their emerging, buoyant wonder.
They make the sign of *more-than-Walrus*,
more than even his own name
for his melting, heavy-hearted self.

BOILING BEETS
for Cindy

You choose them for their solidity and shape, their ability to stain
the heart from under the produce light. Edible greens, too,
the red-veined and cooled trails the morning sun once stalked
in the furrowed fields. You carry them home with other necessities
wrapped in plastic and brown butcher paper, flowers for yourself
in an extravagant fuchsia funnel, reach for beets first out of all
the other chores, charm them to settle together like sleeping children
into one bed, sandy cheeks ruddy with dreams, ignite the fumarole
to flame and will those roots to tremor and roil, your face the moon
rising above earth-steam filling the kitchen, governing the boiling hour.
And when they finally give up their skins and slip between your fingers,
glassy and calm, you follow their growth-rings, a striated map,
with a whetted knife, releasing cross-sections to the jar and pour
vinegar like a salve to preserve their luster. The rubied water swirls
down the drain. Wipe your hands over and over against your apron
but the stain will outlast the rage cooked right out of the pot.

SHADE

The streets are not as sour as the heat
wants us to believe, flags trembling above
used car lots and dogs tethered to a weave
of frayed nerves. Boys snap fireworks
on the court, their quick feet learning
a hard dance. The moon's cool shoulder
turns towards a wilting ice-cream song
rounding the corner, coming close.

As if the bushes were his own,
a man clips roses carefully in the shade
and nestles them like little tropical birds,
getting the arrangement just right
in the green plastic cup spilling water.
Borrowed blooms for his mother, maybe,
or a sweetheart, never knowing how deserving
the man, this street, or the worn rays of sun
have deemed them to be.

SUSPENDED

We take refuge tonight in the stamp-sized park,
summer pooled around our ankles, gratefully cool.
TV sets pulse from living rooms, their muted signals
surrounding us like pearls, underwater.

The public restroom lures lone souls.
Children and men idle like today's cicadas,
the yellow light droning beneath a new moon
and the lost spines of stars. Bats flick the black
canopy of oaks. All moths are welcome.

Two boys on bikes skid up the black-top,
slice the heavy air with their spokes.
They gravitate towards the light.
They call to one another, then swerve
onto the empty soccer field and laugh.

In their wake, a pale kite is dragged
against the darkness. They stir their own
lazy wind, enough to catch nylon and hold
our breath above the inevitable path.

STALK

Their grip closes full round
the thin quill of bamboo
reaching to shoot apart
from the grove that clusters
along the riverbank—a trill of leaves
that will not shake free
no matter how much they lean
their new, upright weight
against this green peer
a wild wrestling
in the wet woods.

Like the fresh page found
exposed on the desk, they slash
a black ballpoint mark
across the words' unfinished face—
make poem, too, mama
toss and train
the stalk to their will,
pricks open the batted sky
to a high blue
a remnant of rain inking
the uncleaved space
in perfect arcs—
Young master,
envious control.

REMNANT

"Eternity is not later, or in any unfindable place.
Roses, roses, roses, roses."

> —Mary Oliver, from "From the Book of Time"

A woman, as young as spring then,
stood in the heart of a muddy pasture
and planted her flags, the roses,
declaring to the cows
and to the strict east wind
this is home, this is where roots
can tap. Like the lilacs, too,
whip-thin and green,
stretching to where their pearls
might cluster and shine,
not these twisted knuckles holding
the cyclone fence to its tilt.

Cornered by cement and brick,
her roses still open.
Two late buds bend demure
in our palms as we lean in
for their rich, old-world perfume,
a bottled-up, forgotten musk.

The small, spotted leaves
cross and uncross themselves
in the spent breeze, hands quaking
to daub a circle of pink rouge
to each cheek, hands not knowing
what else to busy in this tidy,
unfamiliar yard
of someone else's summer.

WEATHERED

Hood up, he drags his feet through the night's puddles, away from the dull fury of mother against father and the duplex containing dogs and his small sister. The gray rain insulates. He watches for the slick yellow bus, its chain-call rounding the feral streets, gathering up children on the first day of school. Nothing keeps him here except the stop-sign at an averted angle, continuously rinsed and red, also taunting the sky. He would rather be out in the sloppy world, soaked by rain unable to find a creek-bed. With his sneaker-heel he carves channels from one pothole to another, and water gratefully follows.

THE TRAJECTORY OF THEIR LEGS

Pedals have been slipping under
a booted will to turn corners,
stretch into longer and longer afternoons.
Not one notch, or two, but three
full clinks the top-tube lengthens.
The bike adjusted, for now,
to this lanky new child-body.

Fingers are counted upon, words slip
from their lips like pigeons spiraling,
white-bellied notes above the wire.
I do nothing but hold
back. These growing pains
are like the stretch-marks
I didn't know I would welcome—
a map to trace the moments
between coming, going,
and soon-to-be gone.

THE HABITS OF HESTIA

There is something about a kitchen full of food
greeting you at 6 a.m.— a greedy comfort—
the coffee pot ready to brew and a tough cut
of beef all night shift-shaping its proteins
in the pickling brine, trading secrets
you thought were only shared
in your long-gone grandmothers' kitchens.

You start the assembling of cabbage wedges,
carrots, onion and oil drizzle, set potatoes and eggs
and beets to boil in their separate copper pots,
each rumbling awake at the same swipe
of the second hand. The family must taste
this cooking-cloud in their dreams.

Your lone cup of coffee.
The radio news is companion
to sharpened knives, oven mitts
and the curtain just parted for clover owling
their faces towards the source.

This might save you, allotting leftovers
for neighbors like a mother-in-law.
The hearth-witch doesn't apologize
for her old-world stove-sauna, for setting fire
to appetites, for waking up the drowsy.
She chips the plates on purpose,
sets the table and waits.

VANISHING POINT

The wind is a steady hand at my chest.
An hour to ride my bike head-first
into spring, that flimsy catkin teasing
from a maple, the thing I follow
at a lumbering, hypnotic cadence,
push through early morning shadows
and winter's left-over gloom
as the sun winnows down the path.
Nothing distracts but the juncos
crisscrossing like lace unraveling.
Behind me, three miles by now,
my child busies the dust
in the hulking house, the place
where all of this began.
I long to be no longer visible, an arrow
quivering into a grove but missing
every tree, an exquisite passing.

Below a frost-slicked trestle,
the creek swells its green skin
with yesterday's pollen and rain.
A fresh grave is being dug on the hill.
Skunk cabbage jaws open above
the curved rot of a lone Chinook
in the shallows. Cottonwood resin
coats the air, sweet and welcome.

From the mottled water, a mallard
pads her way up the mud bank
to a nest enfolded by ten hues of green.
She slips into the tangle
while her mate devotedly treads
in the direction of her return.

Like the expected rioting
of bud to flower to fruit,
I am unable to resist the path.
The wind, now at my back,
chills my bare legs revolving out a rhythm
that will carry me homeward.
Iron-heavy blood floods
its capillarious routes.
Propelled, I become that point
on the horizon eventually
widening back into view.

TRIMMING THE FERNS

One would never think to attempt this in the woods
on slopes where fiddleheads curl out of winter
over the browned forms of their younger selves,
whole sword-tribes thriving, alone, maneuvering
sun-shafts and shadows where mythical giants might kneel
beneath a wild, symmetrical enveloping, the fronds'
under-story not something to be tampered with.

But in the scalloped borders of a tidy city plot
I believe I must trim away the dead to give
the old a surviving chance, steward ancient arms
that have laid centuries of spores, arms that allow
me entry, supplicant palms unfurling, hiding
my black plastic snippers like tricksters
as I ease up from crouching in the duff
from praying, when the night-shade floods.

VOW

You can see the spot
though the body is gone
where the wren dusted her belly,
coating tail feathers, tips of wings,
with soft soot under the old plum.
She pivoted and cupped herself,
rolling over like a horse glad for the grass,
a little joyful winging, then darted
with beak and brow-streak
to the safety of wild grape
coveting the crowded fence.

All day, you will watch over
the small bowl her body tamped
as long as you can tell it apart
from other dry brown bowls,
the places other little brown birds
have carved out for themselves
with strong feather-work.
The ones you will never see.

IN THE TENTH MONTH
for Margot

Most everything is clear.
The night's moon halves
between fir limb and roof pitch
a blue pool spilling
into the steel sink, a shine
that out-weighs streetlamps
and my own turning on.

Midnight rivers and their tributaries
spider down my breasts, down
mountain of baby
covered in parchment
submerged turtle shell
to the shadows carried
in the moment's underbelly.

The white kimono
inked in indigo flowers
no longer closes
the sash atop my ribs
tail of comet
loose end of the script
still spooling over
the page, the quill quivering
before dawn floods
the bearable dark.

WILLIAM STAFFORD SAYS

I have been advised to follow
the thread through my life,
the weathering of the moon,
to not let go—
it pulls me to follow
the course of each day strung
along a necklace of incomprehension,
each imperfect gem against the other,
their sheen loosening.

It tethers the child at the window,
head sweat-curled from sleep
to glasses at rest upon an opened book
to the iron skillet wiped clean with oil,
blue flame snuffed for the night.

I have been advised to watch the full moon
at the equinox, ahead of the weather,
for migrating flocks to pierce its pearly face.
Following their wing-wake,
thread in hand,
I am ready.

BECAUSE MARCH IS A PINK BLOOM
I CAN'T KEEP UP WITH

I keep these moments suspended, green and crowning,
not yet leafed out on the world like a chlorophylling riot,
cottonwoods hazing the pewter skyline, front and back-lit
all at once, the river shedding its otter light, a silver current
its only and forever thought. Let's eddy in the far left lane
of I-5 heading south, the nearly adult child driving
aunt and mother, navigating speed and draft, road ruts
and motorcycles weaving like a video game.
So much I tried to teach my children to look out for.
Potholes and windgusts and the threat of blind-siding.
Bridge after bridge, cliff-towns and container ships stacked
against the opposite bank——I want this river to never
meet its mouth. To be light-locked and stunned.
I want to change the filter to the sepia-green
of their childhood, black-edged and glossy,
each year a full page of calligraphy doodles and buds
breaking loose on the pavement. The magnolia shielding
a flock of starlings. How merciful the tree.
I say, *thank you for driving*, for letting me collapse and watch
a river I love in a warm car full of people I love.
Nick Drake on the radio, our aunt asleep in the backseat,
an open bag of purple-foiled kisses in her lap.
No, not anxious. Just a little sleepy in the Saturday sun.
No rumble strips of worry. Just rolling down the road,
looking for nests, being driven home.

ACKNOWLEDGEMENTS

My gratitude to the editors of the following publications where these poems, in slightly different versions, and with different titles, appeared:

The American Poetry Journal – January at the Duck Pond, Rumor, Suspended, William Stafford Says
CALYX – Staking the Trellis
The Comstock Review – Learning Their Names as They Go, Remnant
Elegant Thorn Review – Grounded, Stalk
Her Circle Ezine – The Habits of Hestia
Hot Metal Press – Boiling Beets, Shade, Trimming the Ferns, Vow, Weathered, When the Moon Floats Unnoticed
Mamazine – They Want to Taste Everything, Stalk
Mom Writers Literary Magazine – The Poem Is the Year
New Letters – Ultrasound
Pilgrimage – Grounded, Vanishing Point
Verseweavers – Moonkilling
VoiceCatcher – Dreaming You While Driving the Columbia, The Habits of Hestia, In the Tenth Month, The Trajectory of Their Legs
Wild Goose Poetry Review – Leveling the Yard at Dusk

For The Willing was first published by Finishing Line Press, 2008, and was nominated by the publisher for the Oregon Book Award.

"Moonkilling" received first place from the Oregon Poetry Association's New Poet's Prize in 2006.

Editions of this chapbook would not have been possible without the support and encouragement of the editors at VoiceCatcher and Finishing Line Press, and Scot Siegel, and early readers, Cindy Mom, Nicholas Manusos, Naomi Berg, and Heather Burns. This collection is dedicated to my children, Alice, and Margot. May they always wander, wonder, and be willing.

ABOUT THE AUTHOR

Kristin Berger is the author of six poetry collections: *Earthwork* (The Poetry Box, 2022), *Changing Man, Changing Woman* (Nightjar Press, 2022), *Refugia* (Persian Pony Press, 2019), *Echolocation* (Cirque Press, 2018), *How Light Reaches Us* (Aldrich Press, 2016), and *For The Willing* (Finishing Line Press, 2008, 1st Edition). She is the recipient of residencies from Playa, OSU/Spring Creek Project's H.J. Andrews Experimental Forest and Shotpouch, and is on the board of directors of Playa at Summer Lake. Originally from Michigan, Kristin lives in Oregon's Willamette Valley. More at kristinbergerpoet.com.

NIGHTJAR POETRY PRESS
Happy Valley, Oregon
Publishing selected poetry books since 2022.
Inquiries, email nightjarpoetrypress@gmail.com.